Prolance

www.prolancewriting.com
California, USA
©2020 Hajar Ashmawey

ISBN: 978-1-7345760-4-7

My First
Surahs

By Hajar Ashmawey
Illustrated by Jenny Reynish

PROLANCE

When I started reading books to my baby, I noticed how he was drawn to the colors and images. Knowing I want to introduce the Quran at a young age and knowing that children are drawn to colors, I decided to write a children's book with Quranic verses and imagery to capture a child's attention during recitation.

As you read the Quran with your child, make sure you take the opportunity to explain to them the meanings of the beautiful words they are reading. Included in this book are just a few of the many lessons I personally want to bring to my child's attention as he grows and learns. The lessons I've chosen are not all-encompassing explanations, and it's important to study the Quran with a trusted source. Be sure to enjoy the journey with your children!

Surah Al-Fatiha

Lesson:
Allah is who we worship and ask for help.

بِسْمِ اللهِ الرَّحْمَنِ الرَّحِيمِ ﴿١﴾

الْحَمْدُ لِلهِ رَبِّ الْعَالَمِينَ ﴿٢﴾

الرَّحْمَنِ الرَّحِيمِ ﴿٣﴾

مَالِكِ يَوْمِ الدِّينِ ﴿٤﴾

إِيَّاكَ نَعْبُدُ وَإِيَّاكَ نَسْتَعِينُ ﴿٥﴾

اهْدِنَا الصِّرَاطَ الْمُسْتَقِيمَ ﴿٦﴾

صِرَاطَ الَّذِينَ أَنْعَمْتَ عَلَيْهِمْ

غَيْرِ الْمَغْضُوبِ عَلَيْهِمْ

وَلَا الضَّالِّينَ ﴿٧﴾

Surah Al-Ikhlas

Lesson:
We can always rely on Allah.

بِسْمِ اللَّهِ الرَّحْمَـٰنِ الرَّحِيمِ

قُلْ هُوَ اللَّهُ أَحَدٌ ﴿١﴾

اللَّهُ الصَّمَدُ ﴿٢﴾

لَمْ يَلِدْ وَلَمْ يُولَدْ ﴿٣﴾

وَلَمْ يَكُن لَّهُ كُفُوًا أَحَدٌ ﴿٤﴾

Surah Al-Falaq

Lesson:
Allah will keep you safe.

بِسْمِ اللَّهِ الرَّحْمَـنِ الرَّحِيمِ

قُلْ أَعُوذُ بِرَبِّ الْفَلَقِ ﴿١﴾

مِن شَرِّ مَا خَلَقَ ﴿٢﴾

وَمِن شَرِّ غَاسِقٍ إِذَا وَقَبَ ﴿٣﴾

وَمِن شَرِّ النَّفَّاثَاتِ فِي الْعُقَدِ ﴿٤﴾

وَمِن شَرِّ حَاسِدٍ إِذَا حَسَدَ ﴿٥﴾

Surah Al-Naas

Lesson:
We need Allah to protect us.

بِسْمِ اللَّهِ الرَّحْمَـٰنِ الرَّحِيمِ

قُلْ أَعُوذُ بِرَبِّ النَّاسِ ①

مَلِكِ النَّاسِ ②

إِلَـٰهِ النَّاسِ ③

مِن شَرِّ الْوَسْوَاسِ الْخَنَّاسِ ④

الَّذِي يُوَسْوِسُ فِي صُدُورِ النَّاسِ ⑤

مِنَ الْجِنَّةِ وَالنَّاسِ ⑥

Surah Al-Asr

Lesson:
Do good things with your time, do not waste it.

بِسْمِ اللَّهِ الرَّحْمَـٰنِ الرَّحِيمِ

وَالْعَصْرِ ﴿١﴾
إِنَّ الْإِنسَانَ لَفِي خُسْرٍ ﴿٢﴾
إِلَّا الَّذِينَ آمَنُوا وَعَمِلُوا الصَّالِحَاتِ
وَتَوَاصَوْا بِالْحَقِّ وَتَوَاصَوْا بِالصَّبْرِ ﴿٣﴾

Surah Al-Kafiroon

بِسْمِ اللَّهِ الرَّحْمَنِ الرَّحِيمِ

قُلْ يَا أَيُّهَا الْكَافِرُونَ ﴿١﴾

لَا أَعْبُدُ مَا تَعْبُدُونَ ﴿٢﴾

وَلَا أَنتُمْ عَابِدُونَ مَا أَعْبُدُ ﴿٣﴾

وَلَا أَنَا عَابِدٌ مَّا عَبَدتُّمْ ﴿٤﴾

وَلَا أَنتُمْ عَابِدُونَ مَا أَعْبُدُ ﴿٥﴾

لَكُمْ دِينُكُمْ وَلِيَ دِينِ ﴿٦﴾

Surah Al-Sharh

بِسْمِ اللَّهِ الرَّحْمَنِ الرَّحِيمِ

أَلَمْ نَشْرَحْ لَكَ صَدْرَكَ ﴿١﴾

وَوَضَعْنَا عَنكَ وِزْرَكَ ﴿٢﴾

الَّذِي أَنقَضَ ظَهْرَكَ ﴿٣﴾

وَرَفَعْنَا لَكَ ذِكْرَكَ ﴿٤﴾

فَإِنَّ مَعَ الْعُسْرِ يُسْرًا ﴿٥﴾

إِنَّ مَعَ الْعُسْرِ يُسْرًا ﴿٦﴾

فَإِذَا فَرَغْتَ فَانصَبْ ﴿٧﴾

وَإِلَى رَبِّكَ فَارْغَب ﴿٨﴾

Hajar Ashmawey currently resides in Dallas, Texas with her family. She is a full time wife, mother, and mental health professional. Hajar earned her Master of Arts in Clinical Mental Health/Counseling from Oakland University in Michigan. She enjoys spending time with her family and working with children.

Jenny Reynish is an artist and illustrator working mainly in children's publishing and has created a wide variety of illustrations for US and UK publishers. Her individual and decorative style was sparked by a Persian rug from Isfahan, inherited from her aunt. She loves the colors and decorative patterns of the Middle East and India, and finds much inspiration from living by the sea. She works in watercolor, oil, and linoprint.
www.magiccarpetpics.co.uk

www.ingramcontent.com/pod-product-compliance
Lightning Source LLC
Chambersburg PA
CBHW060944100426
42813CB00016B/2855